ISLINGTON

Please return this item on or before the last date stamped below or be liable to overdue charges. To renew an item call the number below, or access the online catalogue at www.islington.gov.uk/libraries. You will need your library membership number and PIN number.

KU-288-744

PROBE POWER

HOW SPACE PROBES DO
WHAT HUMANS CAN'T

AILYNN COLLINS

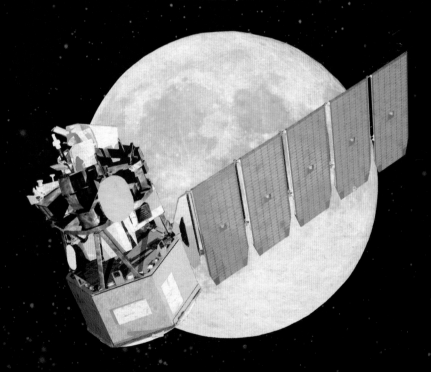

raintree

a Capstone company — publishers for children

Raintree is an imprint of Capstone Global Library Limited, a company incorporated in England and Wales having its registered office at 264 Banbury Road, Oxford, OX2 7DY – Registered company number: 6695582

www.raintree.co.uk
myorders@raintree.co.uk

Text © Capstone Global Library Limited 2020
The moral rights of the proprietor have been asserted.

Editor: Mandy Robbins
Designer: Laura Mitchell
Media researcher: Jo Miller
Original illustrations © Capstone Global Library Limited 2020
Production Specialist: Katy LaVigne
Originated by Capstone Global Library Ltd
Printed and bound in India

ISBN 978 1 4747 8841 0 (hardback)
ISBN 978 1 4747 8851 9 (paperback)

British Library Cataloguing in Publication Data
A full catalogue record for this book is available from the British Library.

Acknowledgements
We would like to thank Sarah Ruiz, an aerospace engineer with NASA, for her invaluable help in the preparation of this book. We would like to thank the following for permission to reproduce photographs: NASA, Cover (Probe), (Probe), 7, 15, 16, Goddard's Conceptual Image Lab/B. Monroe, 28, Johns Hopkins APL/Steve Gribben, 19, APL/Cornell University, 25; Newscom: Cover Images/JAXA etc.., 22, EyePress EPN/ISRO, 17, Photoshot/Bettina Strenske, 21; Shutterstock: Belish, Cover (Moon), 1 (Moon), Cristi Matel, 9, David Herraez Calzada, 12–13, WeAre, 5; Wikimedia: NASA/JHU APL/SwRI/Steve Gribben, 11, NASA/JPL, 27. Design Elements Capstone; Shutterstock: Audrius Birbilas.

CONTENTS

CHAPTER ONE

THE MYSTERY OF SPACE.................................... 4

CHAPTER TWO

SEND IN THE PROBES 6

CHAPTER THREE

INTERPLANETARY PROBES 10

CHAPTER FOUR

ORBITERS 14

CHAPTER FIVE

LANDERS... 20

CHAPTER SIX

WHAT'S NEXT?... 26

GLOSSARY... 30

FIND OUT MORE... 31

WEBSITES 31

INDEX.. 32

CHAPTER ONE

THE MYSTERY OF SPACE

Humans have been curious about space since we first looked up at the night sky. Astronauts have rocketed off Earth and explored outer space. They've stepped foot on the Moon. They've even lived in space at the **International Space Station** (ISS).

Currently, humans can only travel so far. Still, this hasn't stopped scientists from wondering what else is out in the far reaches of space. But how do we discover the mysteries of space if they are too far for humans to get to? We use space probes!

International Space Station place for astronauts to live and work in space

CHAPTER TWO

SEND IN THE PROBES

A space probe is a robotic spacecraft. Rockets launch the probe into space. There are no astronauts on board. The probe is controlled by high-tech computers. It carries special equipment to collect information about what it discovers. Scientists and **engineers** on Earth watch the probe's journey.

A space probe can be as large as a bus or as tiny as a biscuit, depending on its mission. Some probes land on moons or planets. Others take pictures of space objects.

SPACE FACT

The world's smallest space probe is called Sprite. It is the size of a biscuit. It is 644 kilometres (400 miles) above us, orbiting the Earth.

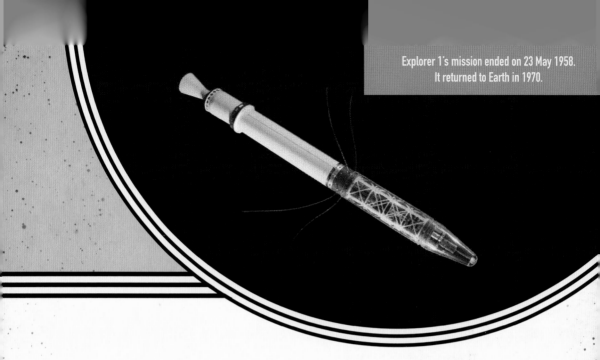

Explorer 1's mission ended on 23 May 1958.
It returned to Earth in 1970.

Countries all around the world have sent probes into space, including the United States, Russia, China, France and India. The first space probe sent into **orbit** was Sputnik 1. The Soviet Union, which later became Russia, launched Sputnik 1 in 1957. A few months later, NASA sent the probe Explorer 1 into orbit. All of these early probes studied Earth from space.

SPACE FACT

NASA stands for the National Aeronautics and Space Administration. Its headquarters is in Washington DC, USA.

engineer someone trained to design and build machines, vehicles, bridges, roads and other structures

orbit path an object follows as it goes around the Sun or a planet

7

A PROBE'S JOB

As technology advanced, scientists sent probes further into space to study other planets, moons and **asteroids**.

Today there are three kinds of space probes – interplanetary probes, orbiters and landers. Some probes have powerful telescopes to study far-away stars and planets. Some fly around in space, while others orbit one object. Still others land on planets and conduct experiments.

Space probes must be able to withstand extreme environments and function properly for long periods of time. Not all probes are successful. Some crash into the object they're supposed to land on. Some simply don't work. But scientists learn from these mistakes. They continue to make better spacecraft for the future.

asteroid a chunk of rock that orbits the Sun; asteroids are too small to be called planets

An orbiter probe travels around Earth.

CHAPTER THREE

INTERPLANETARY PROBES

Interplanetary probes fly past objects in space. These objects can be planets, moons, stars, asteroids or objects we haven't discovered yet. As it flies by, the probe captures images. It also gathers information about the material the object is made of, as well as the object's shape, size and **atmosphere**.

One of the most exciting interplanetary probes in space today is New Horizons. The probe flew past the **dwarf planet** Pluto in 2015. New Horizons was the first probe to study Pluto up close. After this mission ended, the probe went on to study objects in the Kuiper Belt. This area is beyond Neptune. It contains space rocks and other icy objects.

atmosphere layer of gases that surrounds some planets, dwarf planets and moons

dwarf planet space sphere that orbits the Sun but has not cleared the orbit of neighbouring planets

The New Horizons probe collected information from Pluto.

Scientists want to know what kind of material is in the Kuiper Belt. They've made educated guesses but they don't know for sure. Scientists also want to study the rocks that float nearby. One of those space rocks is called Ultima Thule.

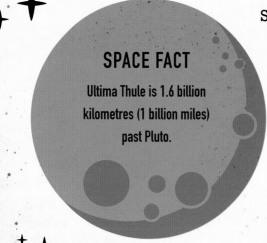

SPACE FACT

Ultima Thule is 1.6 billion kilometres (1 billion miles) past Pluto.

The Madrid Deep Space communication complex is part of NASA's Deep Space Network.

On 1 January 2019, New Horizons made contact with Earth, confirming it had flown by Ultima Thule. This is the furthest that any probe has travelled to explore a planetary body. When New Horizons sent images back to Earth, scientists saw the first pictures of this far-away space rock.

SPACE FACT

New Horizons's radio message was picked up by NASA's Deep Space Network antenna in Madrid, Spain.

CHAPTER FOUR

ORBITERS

Orbiter probes are designed to collect data from a certain planet or moon. Orbiters travel around their object, take pictures and send the information back to scientists on Earth.

The Hubble Space Telescope is an orbiter. It is the size of a minibus and weighs as much as two elephants. The Hubble has been orbiting Earth for almost 30 years, taking pictures of distant stars and objects in deep space. Soon its mission will end.

A new space telescope will begin its mission in 2021. The James Webb Space Telescope will orbit the Sun. It is bigger than the Hubble and will help scientists see even more of the universe. The James Webb will study **black holes**. Hopefully it will send back pictures of objects that we've never seen before.

Other orbiters have been studying planets in our **solar system**. NASA, together with two European space agencies, launched the Cassini probe in 1997. Cassini began to orbit the planet Saturn in 2004. It was the biggest and most expensive probe ever launched.

Cassini studied Saturn and its icy moons for more than 10 years. It travelled 7.9 billion kilometres (4.9 billion miles) and orbited Saturn 294 times.

black hole area of space with such a strong gravitational field that not even light can escape it

solar system the Sun and all the planets, moons, comets and smaller bodies orbiting it

15

The Japanese probe Akatsuki began orbiting the planet Venus in 2015. Earth and Venus are often called twin planets. They are about the same size. They were also formed around the same time. But the planets are very different. The surface of Venus is too hot for humans to survive. Earth's atmosphere has oxygen, which humans need to live. Akatsuki is studying Venus' atmosphere, which is mostly carbon dioxide. It also has clouds made of sulphuric acid, a dangerous chemical for humans.

The Akatsuki probe studied the thick clouds that cover Venus.

The Mangalyaan probe has been orbiting Mars since 24 September 2014.

In 2013 India became the fourth country to successfully send a probe to Mars. Its probe is called Mars Orbiter Mission, or Mangalyaan. Using this probe, scientists are studying Mars's atmosphere and surface. India hopes to have more missions to Mars. One day it may send astronauts to explore the planet.

SPACE FACT

Mangalyaan means "Mars craft" in Sanskrit. Sanskrit is an ancient Indian language.

Scientists study the Sun and how it affects planets. Earth is 149 kilometres (93 million miles) away from the Sun. Getting closer to the Sun's surface will help scientists learn more about it. On 4 November 4 2018, the Parker Solar Probe got closer to the Sun than any other human-made object before it. By 2024 the probe will be even closer – 6.2 million km (3.83 million miles) away.

To stay in one piece, Parker has to withstand an incredible heat of about 1,370 degrees Celsius (2,500 degrees Fahrenheit). That's about 25 times hotter than a hot summer's day on Earth!

The Parker Solar Probe was built with a shield to protect it from the Sun's heat. It also has a cooling system to keep its equipment safe. Scientists believe this probe will show them what happens on the Sun's surface and how **solar flares** affect Earth.

solar flare gas that shoots out of the Sun's surface

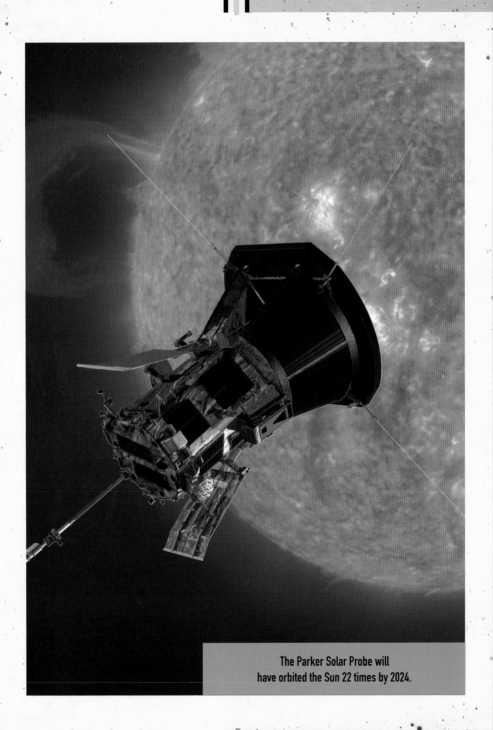

The Parker Solar Probe will
have orbited the Sun 22 times by 2024.

CHAPTER FIVE

LANDERS

A lander is a robotic craft that lands on an object in space. The first probe to ever touch down on another planet was Russia's Venera 7. The probe crashed on Venus's surface on 15 December 1970. For 23 minutes, Venera 7 sent data back to Earth. Then it stopped working. It is still there today.

SPACE FACT

When the Cassini probe was launched in 1997, Europe's Huygens lander hitched a lift. Huygens landed on Titan, one of Saturn's moons.

A failed mission

In 2015 the European Space Agency sent its lander Philae to study a comet. But Philae didn't land on the correct spot on the comet. Scientists lost its signal. Eventually, Philae was found when another probe took a photo of it. Philae had stopped working. It was stuck in a hole on the comet's surface.

In 2015 a model of the Venera 7 lander and parachute was displayed at The Science Museum in London.

NASA's latest lander touched down on Mars on 26 November 2018. InSight is equipped with instruments to measure temperature, wind and even earthquake activity. InSight was accompanied by two miniature **satellites** called Mars Cube One, or MarCO. These satellites relayed information from the probe back to Earth.

SPACE FACT

The MarCO satellites are nicknamed EVE and WALL-E, after characters in the 2008 Pixar film *WALL-E*.

satellite spacecraft used to send signals and information from one place to another

The Hayabusa2 rovers, known as Rover 1A and Rover 1B, move around Ryugu by hopping. This is due to the asteroid's low gravity.

SPACE FACT

Rovers study the rocks and soil of a planet. This gives scientists information about how the planet was formed and if it ever had water.

Landers can be used only once. After they land on the space object, there are no rockets to get them back to Earth. In 2014 the Japanese space agency JAXA launched a special probe called the Hayabusa2. This probe was designed to return after its mission.

In June 2018 the Hayabusa2 reached an asteroid called Ryugu. Hayabusa2 has four rovers on board. Rovers are landers that explore, or rove, a planet's surface. Three of the rovers are on Ryugu, collecting information. The last one is scheduled to land in 2019. In time, Hayabusa2 will create a crater on Ryugu. Then it will collect the loose rocks and dust. At the end of its mission, Hayabusa2's re-entry capsule will return to Earth with samples from Ryugu.

NASA launched two robot rovers called Spirit and Opportunity in 2003. They landed on different parts of Mars. This way scientists could study as much of the planet as possible. Their mission was to look for water. Humans need water to survive. If Mars has water, maybe humans could live there one day.

Spirit and Opportunity took a lot of colourful photos of Mars. Scientists discovered that Mars may have had water a long time ago. But it doesn't any more.

Curiosity is another NASA Mars rover. Launched in 2011, it is collecting rocks and filming the planet's dust storms.

These Mars rovers are not designed to return to Earth on their own. But perhaps someday in the near future, astronauts will be able to walk on Mars and bring these rovers home.

SPACE FACT

The Opportunity rover's mission ended on 13 February 2019. It was the longest-serving rover in NASA history.

CHAPTER SIX

WHAT'S NEXT?

NASA launched the Voyager 1 and Voyager 2 probes in 1977. Their mission was to fly near the outer planets of our solar system – Jupiter, Saturn, Uranus and Neptune. They took pictures of these planets and their moons. No one on Earth had ever seen pictures like these. Soon after, the cameras on the Voyager probes were turned off to save energy. But some instruments are still working.

SPACE FACT

The Voyager probes are carrying messages from Earth. If the probes come across other life forms in space, these recordings could tell them about us and our planet.

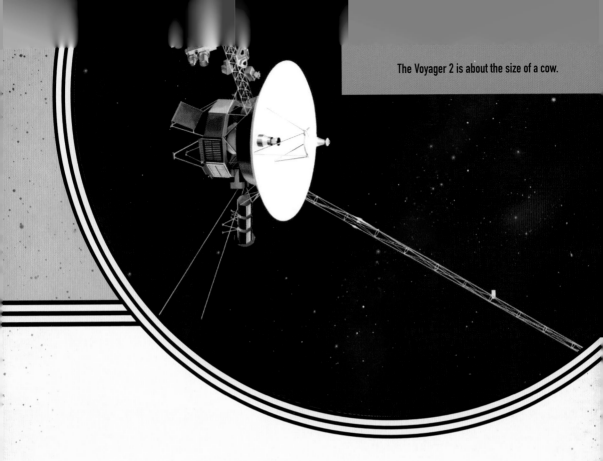

The Voyager 2 is about the size of a cow.

In 2012 Voyager 1 became the first human-made object to fly into **interstellar** space. This is the part of space that is beyond our Sun's magnetic field. Voyager 2 crossed into interstellar space in November 2018. Scientists are now learning more about space just beyond our solar system.

These probes have been in space for more than 40 years. They will keep going until their power runs out. Who knows what else they will find out there.

interstellar between stars, most often used to describe travel from one star to another

ICON will study the ionosphere about 560 km (350 miles) above Earth.

Countries around the world will continue to launch probes into space. European and Russian space agencies are working together to send the ExoMars rover to Mars in 2020. This lander's mission will be to look for signs of life on the planet. It will carry a drill to collect rock and mineral samples and return them to scientists on Earth.

India's Chandrayaan 2 probe will be heading to the Moon in 2019. This probe has a lander, rover and an orbiter. Once Chandrayaan 2 reaches the Moon, the lander and rover will separate from the orbiter and land on the Moon's surface. Then the rover will explore the Moon.

Soon NASA will launch the Ionospheric Connection Explorer (ICON). It will orbit Earth and study the **ionosphere**. This will help scientists protect communication systems and technology in space. They will also learn more about this section of Earth's atmosphere.

Whatever their mission, space probes can do what humans can't. They can travel great distances and spend years in space. The information they gather will be useful for future space programmes. Someday humans may even live on other planets because of the information learned from probes.

ionosphere layer of Earth's atmosphere; the ionosphere is 80 to 966 km (50 to 600 miles) above Earth's surface

GLOSSARY

asteroid   chunk of rock that orbits the Sun; asteroids are too small to be called planets

atmosphere layer of gases that surrounds some planets, dwarf planets and moons

black hole area of space with such a strong gravitational field that not even light can escape it

dwarf planet space sphere that orbits the Sun but has not cleared the orbit of neighbouring planets

engineer someone trained to design and build machines, vehicles, bridges, roads and other structures

International Space Station place for astronauts to live and work in space

interstellar between stars, most often used to describe travel from one star to another

ionosphere layer of Earth's atmosphere; the ionosphere is 80 to 966 km (50 to 600 miles) above Earth's surface

orbit path an object follows as it goes around the Sun or a planet

satellite spacecraft used to send signals and information from one place to another

solar flare gas that shoots out of the Sun's surface

solar system the Sun and all the planets, moons, comets and smaller bodies orbiting it

FIND OUT MORE

Mars Rover Driver (Coolest Jobs on the Planet), Scott Maxwell (Raintree, 2015)

Space Discoveries (Marvellous Discoveries), Tamra B. Orr (Raintree, 2018)

Space Technology: Landers, Space Tourism and More (STEM in Our World), John Wood (Raintree, 2018)

Space Travel (DKfindout), DK (Dorling Kindersley, 2019)

WEBSITES

NASA on the Hubble Space Telescope
www.nasa.gov/audience/forstudents/k-4/stories/nasa-knows/what-is-the-hubble-space-telecope-k4.html

NASA Jet Propulsion Laboratory
www.nasa.gov/centers/jpl/education/spaceprobe-20100225.html

Space Probes
starchild.gsfc.nasa.gov/docs/StarChild/space_level1/probes.html

INDEX

Akatsuki 16

black holes 14

Cassini 15
Chandrayaan 2, 29
Curiosity 24

ExoMars 28
Explorer 1 7

Hayabusa 2 23
Hubble Space Telescope 14

ICON 29
India 7, 17, 29
InSight 21
International Space Station 4

James Webb Space Telescope 14
Jupiter 26

Kuiper Belt 10, 12

Mangalyaan 17
MarCO 21

NASA 7, 15, 21, 24, 26, 29
Neptune 10, 26
New Horizons 10, 13

Opportunity 24

Parker Solar Probe 18
Philae 20
Pluto 10

Russia 7, 20, 28
Ryugu 23

Saturn 15, 26
Spirit 24
Sputnik 1 7

Ultima Thule 12, 13
Uranus 26

Venera 7 20
Venus 16, 20
Voyager 1 26, 27
Voyager 2 26, 27